TECHNOLOGIES
AND
STRATEGIES
IN BATTLE

THE BATTLE OF
MIDWAY

John A. Torres

Mitchell Lane
PUBLISHERS

P.O. Box 196
Hockessin, Delaware 19707
Visit us on the web: www.mitchelllane.com
Comments? email us: mitchelllane@mitchelllane.com

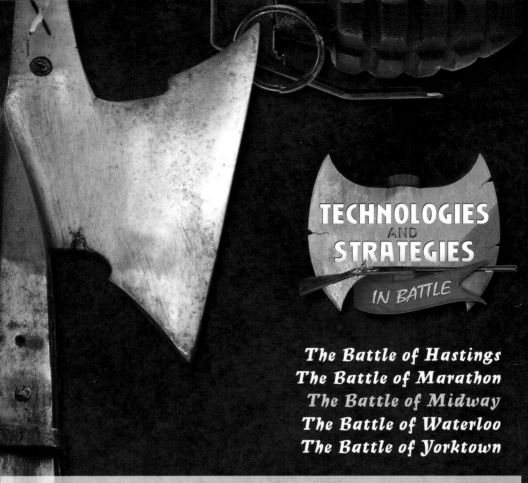

TECHNOLOGIES AND STRATEGIES IN BATTLE

The Battle of Hastings
The Battle of Marathon
The Battle of Midway
The Battle of Waterloo
The Battle of Yorktown

Printing   1   2   3   4   5   6   7   8   9

PUBLISHER'S NOTE: The facts on which the story in this book is based have been thoroughly researched. Documentation of such research can be found on page 45. While every possible effort has been made to ensure accuracy, the publisher will not assume liability for damages caused by inaccuracies in the data, and makes no warranty on the accuracy of the information contained herein.

                                        PLB

Library of Congress
Cataloging-in-Publication Data
Torres, John Albert.
  The Battle of Midway / by John A. Torres.
     p. cm. — (Technologies and strategies in battle)
  Includes bibliographical references and index.
  ISBN 978-1-61228-078-3 (library bound)
  1. Midway, Battle of, 1942—Juvenile literature.
I. Title.
  D774.M5T67 2011
  940.54'26699—dc22
                                        2011002746
eBook ISBN: 9781612281605

ABOUT THE AUTHOR: Seasoned journalist John A. Torres has written many books for Mitchell Lane Publishers, including *We Visit the Dominican Republic*. He lives in Florida with his family.

CONTENTS

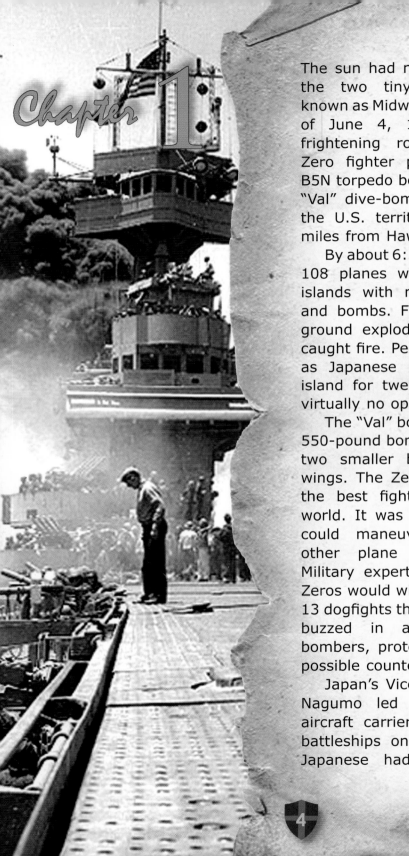

The sun had not yet risen over the two tiny Pacific islands known as Midway on the morning of June 4, 1942, when the frightening roar of Japanese Zero fighter planes, Nakajima B5N torpedo bombers, and Aichi "Val" dive-bombers approached the U.S. territory about 1,300 miles from Hawaii.

By about 6:30 in the morning, 108 planes were spraying the islands with machine gun fire and bombs. Fuel tanks on the ground exploded and buildings caught fire. People ran for cover as Japanese pilots pelted the island for twenty minutes with virtually no opposition.

The "Val" bomber carried one 550-pound bomb in its belly and two smaller bombs under its wings. The Zero was known as the best fighter plane in the world. It was fast, strong, and could maneuver around any other plane it encountered. Military experts have said that Zeros would win 12 out of every 13 dogfights they entered.[1] They buzzed in and around the bombers, protecting them from possible counterattacks.

Japan's Vice Admiral Chuichi Nagumo led a fleet of four aircraft carriers and numerous battleships on the attack. The Japanese had sent 36 Aichi

Attack!

dive-bombers, 36 Nakajima B5N torpedo bombers, and 36 Zero fighter planes.[2] As he normally did when leading an attack, Nagumo kept half of his airplanes in reserve on the ships.

The plan was to destroy all the airfields on the small islands in order to limit what the U.S. planes could do. If the Americans could no longer land on Midway, then the Japanese could easily take over the base. The raid did not go according to plan. The major bombs missed the airfields, and one of the Japanese commanders, Lieutenant Joichi Tomonaga, told his superiors that another round of air strikes would be needed before ground forces could move in.[3]

Some U.S. planes took off from Midway to try to stop the attack. The airmen fought and flew courageously, but their older planes were no match for

Aerial view of the Midway atoll

0   1   2 km
0   1   2 mi

reef

Sand Islet

North Pacific
Ocean

reef

Spit
Island

Eastern
Island

Sand
Island

airfield

reef

reef

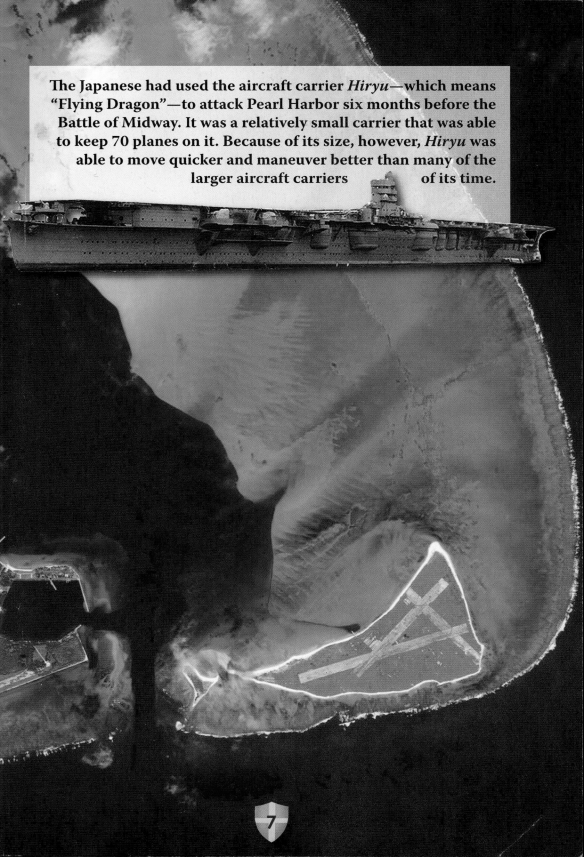

The Japanese had used the aircraft carrier *Hiryu*—which means "Flying Dragon"—to attack Pearl Harbor six months before the Battle of Midway. It was a relatively small carrier that was able to keep 70 planes on it. Because of its size, however, *Hiryu* was able to move quicker and maneuver better than many of the larger aircraft carriers of its time.

the Japanese fighter planes. They managed to drop a few torpedoes in the water, but they scored no major hits on the Japanese. The sky over Midway grew black with smoke. Losing Midway, a strategic American military base, would be devastating for the United States.

The attack was going well, and Nagumo could feel victory close at hand. Instead of keeping the planes prepared to do battle with any U.S. naval ships they might encounter, he ordered them to be refueled and equipped with more bombs to attack Midway. This decision would prove to be a grave tactical error.

Japan had a superior military with a navy that was considered the best in the world. Its leaders planned to take Midway and then take over the Hawaiian Islands. There seemed to be no stopping the spread of the Japanese Empire.

What Japan's leaders did not know was that they were doing exactly what U.S. forces wanted them to do. In a deadly and strategically advanced game of cat and mouse, the Battle of Midway would become the rallying cry for U.S. forces and the first blemish on a seasoned and battle-tested Japanese military.

For months, the American people had waited for the U.S. military to exact some measure of revenge against the Japanese for what they had done to U.S. forces on December 7, 1941. That morning, on the day described by U.S. President Franklin Delano Roosevelt as one that would "go down in infamy," a massive Japanese fleet conducted a surprise attack on the U.S. naval base at Pearl Harbor in Hawaii. The attack consisted of 353 Japanese airplanes that took off from six aircraft carriers, as well as a submarine fleet whose mission was to sink any American warships that escaped from Pearl Harbor and headed to open waters.

The U.S. suffered many losses at Pearl Harbor. In all, 2,403 Americans were killed and nearly 1,200 wounded. The Japanese sank four U.S. battleships, three destroyers, and several other ships. Amazingly, none of the U.S. aircraft carriers were in port that morning—something that would later haunt the Japanese.

The U.S. declared war on Japan the following day, bringing the United States into World War II.

The first major battle between the two world powers took place at a strategically important but little known set of islands known as Midway. While Nagumo was ordering his reserve planes to be fueled and equipped, he had no idea that lurking only 200 miles to the east of Midway were three American aircraft carriers poised and ready to strike a critical blow to the Japanese navy. About three hours after the first Japanese planes were launched

The Japanese *Kaiten* (above) is a one-man suicide torpedo. It was developed from the Type 93 torpedo, nicknamed the Long Lance, and was first used in 1944. These torpedoes gave the Japanese a huge technological advantage over their enemies. Unlike U.S. torpedoes, which left a visible trail of bubbles behind them and often failed to explode, Japanese torpedoes were fueled with pure oxygen, so they did not produce bubbles. Enemy sailors did not know they were coming until their ship was hit.

The aircraft carrier USS *Enterprise* could field 90 aircraft, including fighters, dive-bombers, and torpedo bombers. It was equipped with 12 cannons and 24 heavy-caliber antiaircraft machine guns.

At 6,000 tons, the USS *Atlanta* was considered a light cruiser.

It was fitted with eight 5-inch gun turrets; each gun could fire 15 to 20 rounds per minute. At the Battle of Midway, the *Atlanta* screened the USS *Hornet*.

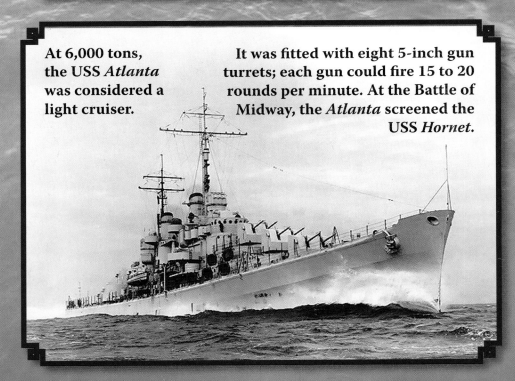

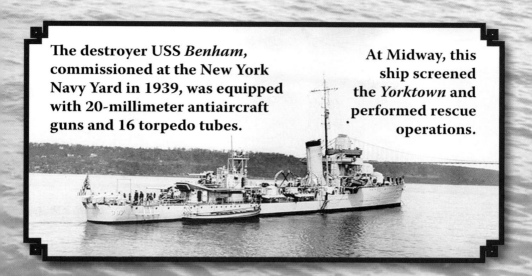

The destroyer USS *Benham*, commissioned at the New York Navy Yard in 1939, was equipped with 20-millimeter antiaircraft guns and 16 torpedo tubes.

At Midway, this ship screened the *Yorktown* and performed rescue operations.

PT (patrol torpedo) boats targeted large surface ships with their torpedoes, and smaller ships with their deck-mounted machine guns.

A 20-millimeter automatic cannon was mounted on the stern. Groups of these fast ships were called mosquito fleets.

The *Yamato*, the flagship of the Japanese fleet, was the largest battleship ever built. Its nine main guns shot shells that were 18 inches (45.7 centimeters) in diameter to a range of 25 miles (40 kilometers).

The USS *Arizona* was sunk during the December 7, 1941, attack on Pearl Harbor. The U.S. officially entered World War II the following day.

and on their way to Midway, the USS *Yorktown*, *Enterprise*, and *Hornet* had launched dive-bombers, torpedo planes, and fighters to the area.

Even though their initial runs at the Japanese ships did not strike any hits, the element of surprise had worked in favor of the United States. Instead of being in attack mode, the Japanese navy found itself having to regroup and go on the defensive.

The Japanese must have wondered how the Americans had known they were planning to strike Midway. The answer was JN-25.

The Japanese Zero

One of the most effective Japanese weapons during the Battle of Midway was a plane known to Americans and their allies as the Zero. This very light, quick, and highly maneuverable plane was actually a Mitsubishi A6M2 Zero. It was first introduced in 1940 and was used during conflicts with China. According to Japanese accounts, in two years of battles with China, only two Japanese Zeros were lost in battle, while they were credited with shooting down 104 Chinese airplanes. The Zeros were used extensively in World War II, including the attack on Pearl Harbor.

The planes had few flaws. They were equipped with two cannons and two machine guns, and they could go long distances—up to 1,930 miles (3,100 kilometers)—without having to refuel.[4] The plane was also very aerodynamic (there was limited resistance from the wind when it flew). Pilots said it was very easy to fly.

The key to such a remarkable and efficient airplane was in its construction. The Japanese used a single piece of lightweight aluminum for each wing. However, because it was so light, it was not able to withstand a lot of hits from machine guns, other planes, or antiaircraft guns. It also could not dive as fast as the heavier U.S. planes.

Japanese Zero fighter plane

Chapter 2

The Japanese attack on Pearl Harbor had served as a wake-up call to the U.S. military and the American people. Never before had a country caught the United States by surprise and delivered such a devastating blow.

After Pearl Harbor, there was a renewed effort to listen in on different radio frequencies and have code-breaking experts, known as cryptanalysts, try to figure out what the Japanese were doing. The Japanese had developed a code or secret language that they thought only they understood.

U.S. code breakers went to work in the Pacific, trying to decipher the communications. They named the Japanese code JN-25, which stood for "Japanese Navy 25." After a lot of hard work, they cracked the code. They realized that the Japanese had put a five-number code to more than 30,000 words. For example, the code for *submarine* was 97850. In order to keep their codes a secret, the Japanese started making them even more complicated.

The main code breakers worked in a basement in Pearl Harbor under the leadership of Commander Joseph Rochefort. Rochefort had lived in Japan for twelve years, so he could speak

Code Breakers

Japanese fluently and was very familiar with the culture. He was more of a mathematician than a soldier. Known as a workaholic, he refused to rest until the code was broken. He slept on a cot in the office, urging his men to work twelve-hour shifts to help crack the code faster. What helped his staff was that most naval transmissions began with the name of the ship that was sending the message, followed by the name of the commanding officer aboard that ship.

Rochefort's team had help from Dutch and British code breakers as well, who worked in other parts of the world. These allied countries shared the information and the radio transmissions they intercepted.

In a technological break-through, Lieutenant Commander Thomas Dyer—one of Rochefort's code breakers—modified an automatic tabulating machine

Joseph J. Rochefort joined the navy after high school and became an engineering officer. The white uniform shown here was used only for ceremonies. After his death, he was awarded two medals for his World War II service: the Navy Distinguished Service Medal and the Presidential Medal of Freedom.

Admiral Nagumo was highly decorated, winning many medals for previous battles, including the attack on Pearl Harbor. The red sash was a sign of luck and was supposed to keep officers protected from gunfire. The sword represented both a badge and a rank.

rented from IBM that would punch the codes onto a card. This allowed the men to mathematically analyze the patterns in the cards.[1]

Still, time was running out. The American military knew the Japanese would strike again, but they did not know where or when. By April 1942, the code breakers had figured out about 30 percent of the Japanese code. They learned the Japanese would be launching an attack on Australian positions in the Coral Sea. The United States responded but was badly defeated in the Battle of the Coral Sea, with the aircraft carrier USS *Yorktown* severely damaged.

The code breakers needed more information. They had a feeling that Japanese radio traffic was talking of attacking Midway, but they couldn't be sure. They laid a trap, and the Japanese fell for it. American forces sent out a radio message to their own headquarters saying that special water purifying machines on Midway had stopped working and that there was not enough freshwater available to drink.

Then they waited and listened. Sure enough, the code breakers soon heard Japanese transmissions talking about bringing water purifiers to the point of attack. Now the Americans were sure that the Japanese would assault Midway, and they knew when.

Nagumo, who led the attack on Pearl Harbor, was hoping to use strategy as well. He was upset that all the U.S. aircraft carriers had survived the attack on Pearl Harbor. His new plan was to attack Midway, hoping the U.S. carriers would steam from Pearl Harbor and face his fleet. He had no way of knowing that the carriers would already be at Midway, waiting for him to send his first wave of planes so that they could destroy his ships.

Because the Americans knew the details of the attack, they sped up repairs to the USS *Yorktown*. U.S. forces worked around the clock to make the ship seaworthy once again. The fact that the *Yorktown* was able to go to battle was a minor miracle.

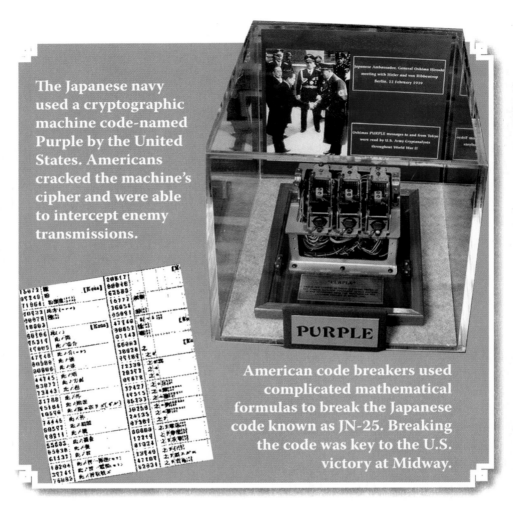

The Japanese navy used a cryptographic machine code-named Purple by the United States. Americans cracked the machine's cipher and were able to intercept enemy transmissions.

PURPLE

American code breakers used complicated mathematical formulas to break the Japanese code known as JN-25. Breaking the code was key to the U.S. victory at Midway.

What was even more important, from a strategic standpoint, was that now its crew knew how to repair a damaged ship.

The code breakers had done their job, and without a second to spare. The Japanese changed their codes just a few days before the attack on Midway began. In the weeks leading up to the attack, Rochefort's men worked all day long deciphering more than 140 radio transmissions per day. The information was given to Admiral Chester W. Nimitz, commander in chief of the U.S. Pacific Fleet. He would set the strategy and try to figure out a way to beat the Japanese at Midway.

Radio Transmissions and Codes

Throughout World War II, the Allied forces—which included the United States—had Joes all over the world. "Joe" was the name given to secret agents running radio transmissions to relay information. Many times, the agents in enemy countries were natives of that land who were angry about what their country was doing. The U.S., for example, had German Joes broadcasting from Germany to Allied troops in Europe.

The agents would be given specific times and special codes to use for their radio transmissions. They would relay whatever information they had about supplies, troop movements, or even no activity. It was very common at that time to change radio frequencies every week and to give the agents a large broadcast area so that they would not be arrested.

Some radio operators worked alone. They had to appear to be living normal, ordinary lives, but they kept quiet and spent much of their time in hiding. They were often referred to as singletons.

If the agents were operating in foreign enemy cities, it was common to have teams of agents on the streets and on rooftops keeping watch to make sure they were not detected. Each of these operators was nicknamed City Mouse. An operator in a rural setting was Country Mouse.[2]

B2 spy transmitter-receiver

Chapter 3

As the Battle of Midway started, the Japanese were feeling confident. The Imperial Japanese Navy was regarded as the best in the world and routinely did as it pleased. It had spent the previous years patrolling the oceans and slowly expanding Japan's sphere of influence. During the previous few decades, Japan had expanded its empire to include Indonesia, Thailand, Burma, the Philippines, Taiwan, Manchuria, and part of China. It had even gained control of two islands in the Aleutian chain, which is part of Alaska. The sailors of the U.S. Navy, which had been crippled at Pearl Harbor, were nowhere near as seasoned as the Japanese.

A little while after Nagumo ordered the refueling and rearming of planes to make another run at Midway, a Japanese scout plane spotted the U.S. aircraft carriers a few hundred miles away. Now Nagumo was faced with a difficult decision. Should he continue with his plans and let his battleships handle the U.S. ships, or should he change strategy and send his planes toward the enemy carriers?

Nagumo ordered the planes to be fueled and then equipped

Naval Maneuvers

with torpedoes and anti-ship guns to take out the U.S. aircraft carriers once and for all. However, this would be time-consuming. The pilot had not marked the exact location when he first spotted the ships, and it would be another 40 minutes before the Japanese scout plane would be able to radio their exact location. The extra time would help the Americans.

Knowing that every second would be crucial, Nimitz ordered the first air assault. Torpedo planes took off from the flight decks of the USS *Hornet*, *Enterprise*, and *Yorktown* aircraft carriers. The Japanese believed the *Yorktown* had been sunk during the attack on Pearl Harbor, so the Americans kept the hulking ship behind the rest of the fleet as a sort of surprise.

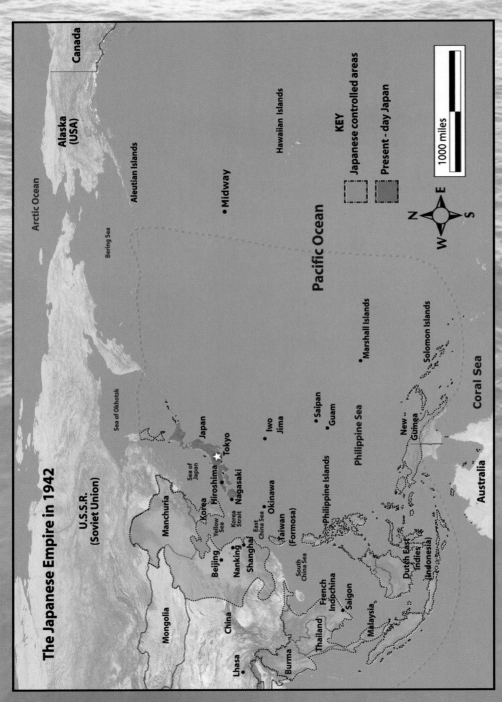

The Japanese Empire in 1942

Canada

Alaska (USA)

Arctic Ocean

Aleutian Islands

Bering Sea

U.S.S.R. (Soviet Union)

Sea of Okhotsk

• Midway

Hawaiian Islands

KEY

Japanese controlled areas

Present - day Japan

N
W — E
S

Pacific Ocean

1000 miles

Sea of Japan

Japan

Tokyo

Hiroshima

Nagasaki

Iwo Jima

• Saipan
• Guam

Marshall Islands

Manchuria

Korea

Yellow Sea

Korea Strait

East China Sea

Okinawa

Taiwan (Formosa)

Philippine Islands

Philippine Sea

Solomon Islands

New Guinea

Mongolia

Beijing

Nanking

Shanghai

China

South China Sea

Lhasa

Burma

Thailand

French Indochina

Saigon

Malaysia

Dutch East Indies (Indonesia)

Australia

Coral Sea

By 1942, Japan had expanded its empire to include eastern Asia and parts of the Pacific, including some of Alaska's Aleutian Islands. When it attacked Hawaii, the U.S. entered World War II against Japan and its allies.

Junior Task Force Commander Raymond Spruance wanted to stagger the U.S. air attack on the Japanese. Although the attacking planes would not be as effective because they would be arriving at different times, he thought it would keep the Japanese occupied longer than a full onslaught would. If they were busy enough, they would not have time to launch a counterattack.

The U.S. bombers were flying without their typical fighter plane escorts and took heavy losses. Japanese fighter planes, already patrolling the sky, found the slow-flying U.S. bombers and attacked. Nearly every U.S. plane was shot down, with little or no damage to the Japanese. But the attack did accomplish a few major objectives. Forced to defend their ships and planes, the Japanese had to stop refueling and arming the planes they were planning to send toward the U.S. fleet. As the Japanese carriers took evasive action, moving quickly and turning sharply, they were no longer in a protective formation. The attack also lured the Japanese fighter planes out of position. They could no longer properly protect their aircraft carriers, and they had already used a lot of their fuel.

At about 10:20 that morning, or nearly an hour after the U.S. sent its first planes toward the Japanese fleet, two squadrons of Dauntless SBD (Scout Bomber Douglas) monoplanes from the *Enterprise* and one squadron from the *Yorktown* took to the skies. They were to strike deadly blows on Japanese aircraft carriers. Nimitz hoped that the decks of the Japanese carriers would be filled with planes that he could damage at the same time.

They were. As the U.S. planes approached, they found three Japanese aircraft carriers—*Kaga*, *Soryu*, and *Akagi*—with full flight decks. The Japanese fighter squadrons—made up of Zero planes—were also nowhere close to the fleet, as they had been chasing the staggered American bombers. They were no longer in position to protect their carriers, and they were too low on fuel to fly back and help.

The U.S. Dauntless SBD was the main dive-bombing plane for the Americans during the first part of World War II. Even though it was known as a slow plane, the Dauntless is credited with sinking more Japanese ships than any other plane in the war.

Japanese planes on the aircraft carriers were being prepared for takeoff. Bombs and torpedoes were stacked on the Japanese decks, making the situation even more dangerous for the Japanese. The strategy was working just as the Americans had planned.

Within minutes, torpedoes and bombs from the diving U.S. planes struck fatal blows on the Japanese carriers. U.S. submarines in the area also attacked. The sky filled with smoke as the three gigantic ships caught fire. Would the attacks be enough to cripple the Japanese fleet?

Submarines at Midway

While most of the battle's glory went to the traditional navy ships and airplanes, submarines played a crucial role at the Battle of Midway. Twelve American submarines were assigned to the battle: *Cachalot, Flying Fish, Tambor, Trout, Grayling, Nautilus, Grouper, Dolphin, Gato, Cuttlefish, Gudgeon,* and *Grenadier*.[1]

The U.S. submarines, armed with guns and torpedoes, supported the warships and aircraft carriers. While many of their torpedoes did not explode or missed their targets, U.S. submarines were critical in cutting supply lines to the Japanese. The main targets for submarines were Japanese merchant ships, which carried supplies and fuel for the Japanese armada.

Many American submarines were updated or retrofitted during World War II to make them more efficient. Some had platforms put on them in order to install antiaircraft guns; others underwent changes to their exteriors, making them harder to spot when they surfaced. Other changes included adding radar, increasing motor and engine power, and adding Kingston valves, which were instrumental in helping the submarines dive deeper faster. These valves, which are on the bottom of a submarine, control panels that open or close to allow water into or out of the submarine's ballast tanks.

Grenadier

At Midway, the Japanese had better airplanes, ships, and overall technology than the Americans did. U.S. strategy involved intercepting radio signals and fooling the Japanese into a false sense of security. But to win a battle, in addition to technology and strategy, risks have to be taken, and there is always an element of luck involved. The battle for the control of Midway was no different.

Even though everything seemed to be going just as the Americans had hoped, the squadron of bombers sent to destroy the Japanese aircraft carriers were actually flying way off course and were nowhere near the Japanese fleet. Having launched from the aircraft carrier *Enterprise*, squadron commander C. Wade McClusky was initially following a similar squadron from the *Hornet*. After a while, he realized the *Hornet* squad leader was following a wrong course. He veered off and ordered his planes to follow.

He searched and searched for the Japanese fleet, using a series of semicircles to cover as much ocean as he could. It was a clear day and McClusky and his men should have been able to spot the great ships. Then

Risk and Retribution

McClusky looked at his fuel gauge.

"My next concern was just how far could we go," McClusky wrote in his account of the battle. "We had climbed, heavily loaded, to a high altitude. I knew the planes following were probably using more [fuel] than I was. So, with another quick calculation, I decided to stay on course 315 degrees until 1200, then turn north-eastwardly before making a final decision to terminate the hunt and return to the *Enterprise*."[1]

The squadron was desperately low on fuel, but McClusky pressed on. Finally he noticed a large wake in the water—and there was a Japanese destroyer. The destroyer had become separated from the rest of the fleet when it was chasing the U.S. submarine *Nautilus*.[2] Elated, he knew the ship would lead them to the rest of the Japanese fleet.

Chapter 4

He and his squadron soon found three Japanese aircraft carriers—the *Kaga*, *Soryu*, and *Akagi*—and started pelting them with bombs. The fuel, planes, and ammunition sitting on the decks of the carriers helped the U.S. bombs do even more damage.

"It was 1222 when I started the attack, rolling in a half-roll and coming to a steep 70-degree dive," McClusky continued. "About halfway down, anti-aircraft fire began booming around us."[3]

Up until that point the attack had been a complete surprise. Now the planes would have to ignore their dwindling fuel supply and continue their bombing run while evading the shells exploding around them.

McClusky would later say that one of the reasons he continued on was that he was not sure if his ship, or any U.S. aircraft carrier for that matter, would still be there when he returned. In his mind he had no choice but to continue fighting.[4]

"In the meantime, our bombs began to hit home,"[5] he said, adding that antiaircraft shells were exploding closer and closer to him. He said that avoiding them was a combination of good luck and his skill as a pilot. He used varying altitudes—flying higher and lower—as well as moving right and left, to keep the enemy from judging where he would be next.

The risk McClusky took—continuing to search for the Japanese fleet when his plane was low on fuel and then attacking in the midst of antiaircraft fire—would pay off in a huge way for the Americans. In a matter of hours, the three carriers—the heart of the Japanese fleet—were destroyed. *Kaga* and *Soryu* would sink later that afternoon, and *Akagi* would sink the next morning. McClusky's plane had been hit 55 times, but he and his gunner made it safely back to the *Enterprise*.

Now there was no possible way that the Japanese would be able to win the Battle of Midway, but the fierce-fighting Japanese would not retreat or surrender. In fact, with three of their four carriers out of the picture, the Japanese actually went on the

offensive. They deployed planes from *Hiryu*, the last remaining Japanese carrier.

With U.S. planes on the attack, the U.S. carriers would not be well protected. Scout planes from the *Hiryu* soon spotted the *Yorktown*.

The first wave of fighter planes from the *Hiryu* struck the *Yorktown* with three different bombs, badly damaging the ship's boilers. Given new confidence, the Japanese sent another wave of planes from the *Hiryu*, hoping to destroy a second American aircraft carrier. The fact that the crew of the *Yorktown* was experienced in repairing their ship made a huge difference in the battle. The crew was able to patch up the ship and get it back in working order in a very short time. They did such a great job that by the time the second wave of Japanese planes arrived in the area, the Japanese thought the *Yorktown* was a different carrier. They believed the *Yorktown* had already gone to the bottom of the sea.

The Japanese planes attacked the *Yorktown* again, and this time they damaged the ship too much for repairs to be made at

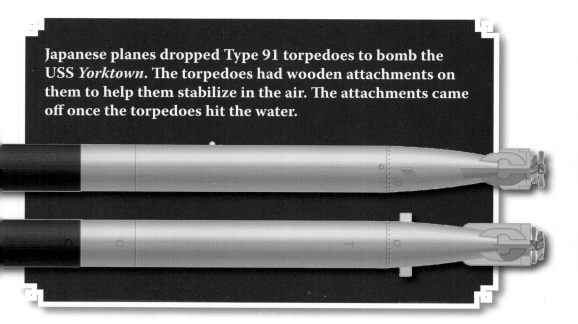

Japanese planes dropped Type 91 torpedoes to bomb the USS *Yorktown*. The torpedoes had wooden attachments on them to help them stabilize in the air. The attachments came off once the torpedoes hit the water.

The USS *Yorktown* is struck on its port (left) side and begins to burn. Meanwhile, the sky is blackened by heavy antiaircraft fire.

Before World War II, battleships and destroyers had conning towers where sailors could look out for enemy vessels. These were replaced with radar and communications towers (above) beginning in the late 1930s.

sea. The command staff and much of the crew were able to get off the ship and onto support vessels nearby. Meanwhile, the Japanese thought that they had disabled two American carriers, when in fact it was only one.

In another stroke of luck, a scout plane from the *Yorktown* spotted the *Hiryu* and radioed its location to the U.S. fleet. It would be a sitting duck for the Americans.

Radar

While the technology was not new, radar was used in battle for the first time in World War II. Radar, short for "*ra*dio *d*etection *a*nd *r*anging," allowed military leaders to figure out the location of enemy ships or planes simply by using radio waves.

In 1887, Heinrich Hertz discovered that radio waves bounced off solid objects. Almost twenty years later, German inventor Christian Hülsmeyer used his primitive radar device to detect a large ship approaching in the fog. His device, however, was not able to detect the ship's distance.

In the years leading up to World War II, many of the world's most powerful countries—including Japan and the United States—developed their own versions of radar. The U.S. installed a large radar antenna on Midway. It allowed the Americans to detect the oncoming Japanese fleet and prepare for an attack. Radar was still bulky then, and not as portable as it would become. Aircraft carriers relied more on scout planes to take to the sky and locate enemy ships than they did on radar. However, military leaders realized that radar was valuable as an alert system. It became a more important part of the military in the months and years that followed.

Today, radar has many applications. Air traffic controllers use it to keep track of planes at busy airports. Meteorologists use it to detect changes in the atmosphere and the paths of big storms, which helps them predict the weather.

Early radar station, 1945

Of the two waves of planes that flew against the *Yorktown* and disabled it, many planes made it safely back to the *Hiryu*. The Japanese had an idea where the remaining U.S. carriers were, so the order was given to refuel and rearm the planes for more attacks against the Americans.

Fleet Admiral Isoroku Yamamoto, nearby on a command ship, knew that this was the only Japanese aircraft carrier left. He also knew that Japanese sailors were more experienced and in many ways better trained than their U.S. counterparts. He thought his forces might be able to defeat the Americans even without the carriers. He radioed the other ships in his fleet and ordered all the battleships and cruisers to his location so that they could launch one more attack, a decisive battle that would put U.S. aircraft carriers out of commission.

Unluckily for Yamamoto, however, U.S. planes spotted the *Hiryu* and were well aware of the ship's location. Once the information was confirmed, a massive U.S. attack was under way. Roughly forty American planes were launched from the *Enterprise* and *Hornet*. The squadron from the *Enterprise*

Resounding Victory

encountered *Hiryu* first and dropped four bombs on the ship's deck, damaging it severely. Later, SBDs dive-bombed the *Hiryu*, scoring several direct hits. Shortly after that, B-17 bombers attacked the Japanese vessel and pelted the ship with machine gun fire.

Though the *Hiryu* was on fire and badly damaged, the ship was still able to move forward. The engines were fine. Yamamoto was not going to give up. In fact, he carried out his plan to attack the U.S. fleet with surface vessels, including battleships and cruisers.

With large guns and torpedoes on board, Yamamoto believed that the battleships could inflict heavy damage on the U.S. carriers and maybe even sink them. The Americans, who had lost their battleships during the attack on Pearl

During World War II, aircraft carriers had a steam-powered catapult to help the planes get enough speed to launch from the short runways. The planes shown below are modern naval aircraft.

Planes landing on aircraft carriers had to snag one of four arresting cables with a tailhook, which is near the back of the plane.

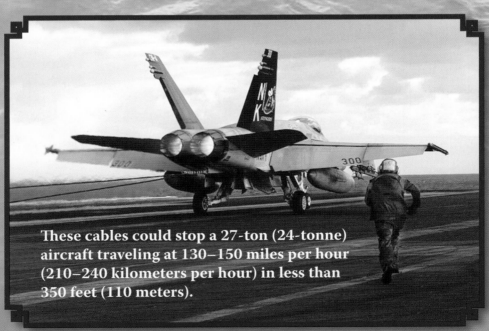

These cables could stop a 27-ton (24-tonne) aircraft traveling at 130–150 miles per hour (210–240 kilometers per hour) in less than 350 feet (110 meters).

Harbor, relied on cruisers and smaller vessels to protect the carriers at sea.

As the numerous Japanese attack ships were closing in, U.S. Commander Spruance ordered his fleet to retreat. He knew that one of the main objectives of naval battles in general is never to allow your aircraft carriers to be in range of enemy guns. This is sometimes easier said than done, but Spruance could not let his carriers fall within range of the oncoming Japanese battleships. Instead of engaging the Japanese, the U.S. ships moved away from them. In fact, for half the night the U.S. fleet continued moving east and then north away from the Japanese.

By midnight, the fires on the *Hiryu* were burning out of control, and after a few explosions, the ship stopped moving. The engines were destroyed. Admiral Tamon Yamaguchi could no longer proceed with his attack.

As the moon shone brightly in the sky, Yamaguchi ordered his crew of 800 to the deck of the ship. He thanked them for their service, and they sang the Japanese national anthem. Then they cheered three times. As rescue boats began to arrive, Yamaguchi ordered the evacuation of the ship.

However, Yamaguchi, who believed in the way of the Samurai warrior, considered it a disgrace to leave his ship. He remained on board even as the aircraft carrier began to sink. About 35 other men, including the ship's captain, Tomeo Kaku, also chose to go down with the ship rather than face the humiliation of having lost the battle. Yamaguchi gave his hat to one of his officers and asked him to deliver it to his family.

According to several accounts, Yamaguchi and Kaku spent their last few moments on the ship talking about the moon.

"Let us enjoy the beauty of the moon," Yamaguchi is reported to have said.

"How bright it shines," Kaku responded.

"It must be in its twenty-first day."[1]

Chapter 5

A torpedo from a Japanese submarine slammed the *Hiryu* to send it to the bottom of the ocean. Scuttling ships and other equipment is a common warfare tactic. It prevents the enemy from learning about the ship's technology and other secret information.

The loss of the ship was not as great as the loss of Yamaguchi. Many experts considered him to be Japan's best naval officer. His death had a crippling effect on the rest of the Japanese forces.

At the first sign of sunlight, the Americans began heading southwest again, back toward Midway, launching scout planes to try to locate the Japanese. The remaining Japanese fleet turned back toward Japan, a defeated force. Spruance's critics said he allowed them to get away instead of crushing their force once and for all. On the other hand, for maneuvering his fleet out of harm's way, he was considered a hero and was awarded the Navy Distinguished Service Medal.

Meanwhile, the crippled *Yorktown* was being towed back to Pearl Harbor. On June 6, a Japanese submarine torpedoed the *Yorktown* and its escort ship, the USS *Hammann*. The *Hammann* sank quickly, and as it did, its armed depth charges detonated. The explosions further damaged the *Yorktown*, and it sank the next day.

The Japanese navy suffered the worst defeat in the country in more than 350 years. The Americans had sunk four aircraft carriers, a cruiser, three destroyers, and an oiler, and they had badly damaged a battleship. The Japanese fleet lost a total of 322 planes. The United States lost one aircraft carrier, one destroyer, and 147 planes.[2]

The Battle of Midway gave Americans something they desperately needed to continue waging a successful war: time. The Americans were now able to control certain parts of the Pacific Ocean while new, better, faster aircraft carriers were being built in the United States.

Ensign George H. Gay was the only survivor in his squadron after the June 4 attack on the Japanese carrier force. He smiles at the news of the U.S. victory at Midway.

The steel-plated hull of Japan's *Yamato* weighed 23,000 tons; but the ship was weaker near the bow and stern, and the torpedoes that struck it there succeeded in sinking the ship.

It also gave the Americans the confidence they needed to defeat Japan. Although the decision to drop nuclear bombs on Hiroshima and Nagasaki would ultimately win the war, the Battle of Midway ended the Japanese dominance of the seas and changed the tide to victory for the Allies.

Aircraft Carriers

More than 100 years before aircraft carriers would become arguably the most valued military technology in World War II, the British were using them to drop leaflets in a propaganda war against French dictator Napoléon Bonaparte. They were also used to carry hot-air balloons, which were sent aloft for observation and mapmaking purposes.

In the early 1900s, the French navy used what are believed to be the first water vessels that carried airplanes. The British soon followed with a ship called the HMS *Hermes* (it was sunk in 1914 by a German submarine). The U.S. Navy introduced its first plane carrier, the USS *Mississippi*, in 1913.

In those days, ships could launch the planes with a catapult, but the planes could not return to land on the ships. Cranes would collect them and place them back on the ships. In 1914, during World War I, both the Japanese and the British navies launched successful strikes using these primitive aircraft carriers. It wasn't until the 1920s, after World War I, that countries began building large ships with takeoff and landing strips on them.

Aircraft carriers have come a long way since the ships used at the Battle of Midway. For instance, with the advent of nuclear power, carriers in the 1960s no longer had to rely on oil-based fuel and could travel farther than before. Later, electro-magnetic technology was developed for catapulting planes off flight decks, and using unmanned aircraft was becoming more common.

USS *Bataan* helicopter carrier

1942

May 27	The Japanese fleet—including four aircraft carriers—leaves Japan and heads for Midway.
May 28	The U.S. force heads for Midway to engage the Japanese fleet.
May 30	The USS *Yorktown* aircraft carrier is repaired from damage incurred at Pearl Harbor. It sets sail to join the rest of the American fleet.

June 4

4:30 a.m.	Both the Japanese and the Americans launch scout planes.
5:55 a.m.	U.S. forces on Midway use radar to detect the Japanese attack force.
6:00 a.m.	All U.S. planes on Midway take off to meet the Japanese attack.
6:30 a.m.	The Japanese attack on Midway begins.
7:10 a.m.	American scout planes locate the Japanese fleet.
8:35 a.m.	The Japanese leaders order the returning planes from Midway to refuel and rearm in order to attack the U.S. ships.
9:25 a.m.	A squadron of planes from the USS *Hornet* is shot down as it attacks Japanese ships.
9:45 a.m.	Unable to locate the Japanese aircraft carriers, a squadron of U.S. bombers led by C. Wade McClusky finds a Japanese ship. It follows from a distance as the ship leads them to the rest of the Japanese fleet.
10:20 a.m.	U.S. planes bomb Japanese aircraft carriers that are still working to refuel and rearm planes on their decks. Three Japanese aircraft carriers—*Akagi*, *Kaga*, and *Soryu*—are destroyed.
11:55 a.m.	The last Japanese aircraft carrier—*Hiryu*—launches planes and successfully bombs the USS *Yorktown*.
1:25 p.m.	The *Yorktown*'s engines are repaired and the ship begins to move.
2:45 p.m.	Thinking they have located another American aircraft carrier, more planes from the *Hiryu* bomb the *Yorktown* again, this time doing more damage. American ships start towing the ship to port.
5:05 p.m.	Planes from the USS *Enterprise* bomb the *Hiryu*.
June 5	At 2:30 a.m., the *Hiryu* sinks with Admiral Tamon Yamaguchi, Captain Tomeo Kaku, and about 35 others aboard.
June 6	A Japanese submarine attacks the *Yorktown* as it is being towed. It sinks the next day.

1854	U.S. Commodore Matthew Perry and his fleet force Japan to open its ports to foreign trade.
1904–1905	Japan defeats Russia in the Japanese-Russo War.
1919	The Treaty of Versailles, which officially ends World War I, is signed on November 11.
1931	The Japanese army invades Manchuria, China.
1932	Franklin D. Roosevelt is elected president of the United States.
1936	In January, Japan withdraws from treaty talks with the United States and Great Britain that would have extended treaties that limited the size of its navy.
1937	Japan wages a full-scale war on China.
1941	On December 7, Japan bombs American ships stationed at Pearl Harbor. The next day, the United States declares war on Japan.
1942	
April 1	The United States begins putting 110,000 Japanese Americans into detention camps.
April 19	Japan takes the Philippine island of Luzon.
May 7	In the Battle of the Coral Sea, the *Yorktown* is badly damaged, but two Japanese carriers are so severely damaged that they will not take part at Midway.
June 4	The United States defeats Japanese forces during the Battle of Midway.
1944	In June, at the Battle of the Philippine Sea, 200 Japanese aircraft are shot down over the Marianas Islands. The U.S. Navy destroys the Japanese navy during the battle of Leyte Gulf on October 26.
1945	
January 9	U.S. forces retake Luzon and establish an air base there.
February 19	U.S. forces invade Iwo Jima.
March 9	U.S. planes firebomb Tokyo, killing 83,000 to 100,000 people.
August 6	U.S. drops an atomic bomb on Hiroshima.
August 9	U.S. drops an atomic bomb on Nagasaki.
August 14	Japan surrenders.
1951	Japan and the United States sign the San Francisco Treaty on September 8. It grants Japan its freedom.
1960	On January 19, Japan and the United States sign the Treaty of Mutual Cooperation and Security, which officially makes the two countries allies; the U.S. stations troops in Japan, including on Okinawa, in order to defend Japan and help maintain peace in Asia and the Pacific.

Chapter 1. Attack!

1. *National Geographic's Battle for Midway* (documentary, 1999); http://www.snagfilms.com/films/title/battle_for_midway/
2. Naval History and Heritage Command: *Battle of Midway, June 4–7, 1942*, http://www.history.navy.mil/photos/events/wwii-pac/midway/midway.htm
3. World War II History Info: *The Battle of Midway*, http://www.worldwar2history.info/Midway/Battle-of-Midway.html
4. Ghost Squadron: "Mitsubishi A6M2 Model 21 Rei-sen (Zero) Japanese Carrier Fighter," http://rwebs.net/ghostsqd/a6m2.htm

Chapter 2. Code Breakers

1. Stephen Budiansky, *Battle of Wits: The Complete Story of Codebreakers in World War II* (New York: Touchstone, 2000); online at http://www.worldwar2history.info/Midway/Battle-of-Midway.html
2. Central Intelligence Agency, "Agent Radio Operation During World War II," released September 22, 1993, https://www.cia.gov/library/center-for-the-study-of-intelligence/kent-csi/vol3no1/html/v03i1a10p_0001.htm

Chapter 3. Naval Maneuvers

1. Department of the Navy, *Battle of Midway*, http://www.history.navy.mil/faqs/faq81-1.htm

Chapter 4. Risk and Retribution

1. LCDR C. Wade McClusky, "Battle of Midway," *USS Enterprise CV-6: The Most Decorated Ship of the Second World War*, http://www.cv6.org/company/accounts/wmcclusky/
2. Stephen Budiansky, *Battle of Wits: The Complete Story of Codebreakers in World War II* (New York: Touchstone, 2000); online at http://www.worldwar2history.info/Midway/Battle-of-Midway.html
3. McClusky.
4. Ibid.
5. Ibid.

Chapter 5. Resounding Victory

1. Peter Chen and the Pacific Campaign, "Tamon Yamaguchi," *World War II Database*, http://ww2db.com/person_bio.php?person_id=39
2. U.S. Navy: "The Course to Midway: Triumph at Midway," http://www.navy.mil/midway/midway_7_TOUHEY_BOOK%20EXCERT.html

Books

Beller, Susan. *Battle in the Pacific: Soldiers in World War II*. Mankato, Minnesota. Lerner Publishing Group, 2008.

Doeden, Matt. *Weapons of World War II*. Mankato, MN: Capstone Press, 2008.

Spencer, Linda. *The War at Home: Japan During World War II*. San Diego: Lucent Books, 2007.

White, Steve, and Richard Elson. *The Battle of Midway: The Destruction of the Japanese Fleet*. New York: Rosen Publishing Group, 2007.

White, Steve, Richard Elson, and Gary Erskine. *The Empire Falls: Battle of Midway*. New York: Rosen Publishing Group, 2006.

Works Consulted

Budiansky, Stephen. *Battle of Wits: The Complete Story of Codebreakers in World War II*. New York: Touchstone, 2000.

Central Intelligence Agency, "Agent Radio Operation During World War II," released September 22, 1993. https://www.cia.gov/library/center-for-the-study-of-intelligence/kent-csi/vol3no1/html/v03i1a10p_0001.htm

Department of the Navy; Naval History and Heritage Command: "The Battle of Midway."
http://www.history.navy.mil/faqs/faq81-1.htm

Department of the Navy; Naval History and Heritage Command: "The Battle of Midway, Overview and Special Image Selection."
http://www.history.navy.mil/photos/events/wwii-pac/midway/midway.htm

EyeWitness to History: "The Battle of Midway, 1942."
http://www.eyewitnesstohistory.com/midway.htm

Insom, Dallas W. *Midway Inquest: Why the Japanese Lost the Battle of Midway*. Bloomington: Indiana University Press, 2007.

Lewis, Susan K. "Anatomy of the Battleship *Yamato*." *NOVA*, December 1, 2009. http://www.pbs.org/wgbh/nova/military/anatomy-yamato.html

Library of Congress, Congressional Record, 111th Congress (2009–2010), Thomas: "Recognizing 50th Anniversary of United States-Japan Treaty of Mutual Cooperation and Security—(House of Representatives—June 23, 2010)." http://thomas.loc.gov/cgi-bin/query/z?r111:H23JN0-0045:

National Geographic's Battle for Midway (documentary, 1999). http://www.snagfilms.com/films/title/battle_for_midway/

National Security Agency: "The Battle of Midway—How Cryptology Enabled the United States to Turn the Tide in the Pacific War." http://www.nsa.gov/about/cryptologic_heritage/center_crypt_history/publications/battle_midway.shtml

Parshall, Jonathan, and Anthony Tully. *Shattered Sword*: *The Untold Story of the Battle of Midway*. Herndon, Virginia: Potomac Books, 2005.

Stille, Mark, and Howard Gerrard. *Midway 1942*: *Turning Point in the Pacific*. Oxford, United Kingdom: Osprey Publishing, 2010.

U.S. Navy: "A Brief History of U.S. Navy Aircraft Carriers: Battle of Midway." http://www.navy.mil/navydata/navy_legacy_hr.asp?id=7

U.S. Navy: "The Course to Midway: Triumph at Midway." http://www. navy.mil/midway/midway_7_TOUHEY_BOOK%20EXCERT.html

World War II History Info: "Midway—Denouement: 'Radio Intelligence' Vindicated." http://www.worldwar2history.info/Midway/intelligence. html

On the Internet

Ace Pilots: "USS *Benham* (DD-397), U.S. Navy Destroyer of World War Two"
http://www.acepilots.com/ships/benham.html

The Aviation History On-Line Museum: "Boeing B-17 Flying Fortress"
http://www.aviation-history.com/boeing/b17.html

Great Aircraft of History: World War Two Airplanes and More
http://www.acepilots.com/planes/main.html

Hawks, Chuck. "Best Fighter Planes of World War II.
http://www.chuckhawks.com/best_fighter_planes.htm

History Learning Site: World War II, "The Battle of Midway"
http://www.historylearningsite.co.uk/battle_of_midway.htm

The National Museum of American History: Submarines in World War II
http://americanhistory.si.edu/subs/history/subsbeforenuc/ww2/

USS *Atlanta* Class—Design History
http://ussatlanta.com/atldesignhistory.htm

USS *Hornet* Museum: "USS *Hornet* During World War II"
http://www.uss-hornet.org/history/wwii/

World War II American Submarine List
http://www.fleetsubmarine.com/sublist.html

World War II: The Battle of Midway
http://www.2worldwar2.com/battle-of-midway.htm

World War II Pacific
http://www.ww2pacific.com/

altitude (AL-tih-tood)—The distance up from the ground.

battleship (BAT-ul-ship)—A large, heavily armored warship that shoots projectiles weighing hundreds of pounds.

cipher (SY-fur)—A message in code.

cruiser (KROO-zur)—A large warship with less armor and lighter guns than a battleship.

cryptanalyst (kript-AN-uh-list)—A specialist in breaking codes.

decipher (dee-SY-fur)—To figure out the hidden meaning of something.

destroyer (dee-STOYR-ur)—A small, swift warship used mainly to escort larger ships and to attack submarines.

devastating (DEH-veh-stay-ting)—Causing ruin.

distinguished (dis-TING-wisht)—Marked by excellence.

evacuation (ee-vak-yoo-AY-shun)—The forced removal of people from a dangerous location.

maneuvers (muh-NOO-vurs)—A series of military movements.

meteorologist (mee-tee-ur-AH-luh-jist)—Someone who observes the weather and makes predictions.

PT boat—Short for *patrol torpedo*, a small, easily maneuverable and very fast boat that carries torpedoes and light guns.

radar (RAY-dahr)—Short for *radio detection and ranging*, a device that uses radio waves to locate distant objects and to judge their speed.

retrofit (REH-troh-fit)—To add instruments, armament, or other accessories to a ship or vehicle after it has left the manufacturing plant.

scuttle (SKUH-tul)—To destroy one's own ship (or other vehicle) on purpose, usually to keep its technology out of enemy hands.

squadron (SKWAH-drun)—A military group or flight formation.

tactical (TAK-tih-kul)—Used in a plan to accomplish a purpose.

terminate (TER-mih-nayt)—To bring something to an end.

wake (WAYK)—The track of waves left in the water by a passing ship.

Index